# Out Of The Whirlwind

*First Lesson Sermons For Sundays After Pentecost (Last Third) Cycle B*

# John A. Stroman

CSS Publishing Company, Inc., Lima, Ohio

OUT OF THE WHIRLWIND

Copyright © 1999 by
CSS Publishing Company, Inc.
Lima, Ohio

All rights reserved. No part of this publication may be reproduced in any manner whatsoever without the prior permission of the publisher, except in the case of brief quotations embodied in critical articles and reviews. Inquiries should be addressed to: Permissions, CSS Publishing Company, Inc., P.O. Box 4503, Lima, Ohio 45802-4503.

Scripture quotations are from the *New Revised Standard Version of the Bible*, copyright 1989 by the Division of Christian Education of the National Council of the Churches of Christ in the USA. Used by permission.

---

**Library of Congress Cataloging-in-Publication Data**

Stroman, John A.
  Out of the whirlwind : first lesson sermons for Sundays after Pentecost (last third), cycle B / John A. Stroman.
        p. cm.
     Includes bibliographical references.
     ISBN 0-7880-1388-2 (pbk. : alk. paper)
     1. Pentecost season Sermons.  2. Catholic Church Sermons.  3. Sermons, American.
I. Title.
BV4300.5.S76      1999
252'.64—dc21                                                                                                99-32555
                                                                                                                        CIP

---

For more information about CSS Publishing Company resources, visit our website at www.csspub.com.

PRINTED IN U.S.A.

*To the members of
Ebenezer Methodist Church,
Madina, Ghana, West Africa,
whose joyful singing and
radiant Christian spirit
I will never forget.*

# Table Of Contents

| | |
|---|---|
| **Introduction** | 7 |
| **Proper 22** <br> **Pentecost 20** <br> **Ordinary Time 27** <br>    Taking The Good With The Bad <br>    Job 1:1; 2:1-10 | 9 |
| **Proper 23** <br> **Pentecost 21** <br> **Ordinary Time 28** <br>    Making Our Feelings Known <br>    Job 23:1-9, 16-17 | 15 |
| **Proper 24** <br> **Pentecost 22** <br> **Ordinary Time 29** <br>    Out Of The Whirlwind <br>    Job 38:1-7 (34-41) | 19 |
| **Proper 25** <br> **Pentecost 23** <br> **Ordinary Time 30** <br>    Confession <br>    Job 42:1-6, 10-17 | 25 |
| **Proper 26** <br> **Pentecost 24** <br> **Ordinary Time 31** <br>    The Tale Of Three Women <br>    Ruth 1:1-18 | 31 |
| **Proper 27** <br> **Pentecost 25** <br> **Ordinary Time 32** <br>    Expanding The Boundaries <br>    Ruth 3:1-5; 4:13-17 | 37 |

**Proper 28**     43
**Pentecost 26**
**Ordinary Time 33**
   God Remembers
   1 Samuel 1:4-20

**Christ The King Sunday**     49
   What's So Great About Jesus?
   2 Samuel 23:1-7

**All Saints' Sunday**     55
   With All The Saints
   Isaiah 25:6-9

**Thanksgiving Day**     61
   Thankful Living
   Joel 2:21-27

**Lectionary Preaching After Pentecost**     67

# Introduction

During the academic year of 1997-98 I was a visiting lecturer in New Testament at Trinity Theological College in Ghana, West Africa. It was during this time that a portion of this work was completed. The students in my class along with laity and clergy in the Methodist Church in Ghana, for whom I have such great respect and appreciation, provided me with both inspiration and insight.

Our text deals with the first lessons of the last third of the Pentecost season bringing to a close the liturgical year. The first four lessons are from Job, dealing with issues that are extremely contemporary. We discover in these texts that Job's struggles are our struggles. The texts from Ruth and 1 Samuel introduce us to four important Old Testament women: Naomi, Orpah, Ruth, and Hannah. They all play an important role in the biblical narrative, as well as providing insight into vital current issues.

Christ the King Sunday brings to a close the church's liturgical year. As one scholar has suggested, the celebration of Christ the King is like the *coda* in a Beethoven symphony. It not only brings the movement to a decisive end, but it forms a climax to what has gone on before. It is both the summing up and something splendidly new. The preacher now has the opportunity to prepare the congregation for one of the greatest celebrations of all — Advent.

John A. Stroman
Tallahassee, Florida

*Proper 22* • *Pentecost 20* • *Ordinary Time 27*

## Taking The Good With The Bad

*Job 1:1; 2:1-10*

---

**Once upon a** time in the land of Uz there was a man whose name was Job. He was a man of sterling character who always sought to do the right thing. Above all he had respect for God and hated evil with a passion. His family consisted of seven sons and three daughters. God had blessed Job not only with a large family but he possessed seven thousand sheep, three thousand camels, five hundred yoke of oxen, five hundred donkeys, and numerous servants who cared for his enormous amount of livestock. He had the respect of all the people in the east and enjoyed not only a good reputation, but he was enjoying the good life. Everything was going Job's way. He seemed to have the Midas touch, turning opportunity into fortune.

Job enjoyed his family. He took pride in them and their accomplishments. Throughout the community he was known as a family man who always had time for his children. On numerous occasions his sons would have cookouts and invite their sisters to come share in the good food, drink, and fellowship. Following their days of feast and celebration Job would rise early in the morning and sacrifice a burnt offering unto the Lord on the behalf of each of them. He did this because he was concerned that possibly one of his children might have cursed God and he wanted to make atonement for any sin they might have committed. In other words, Job was covering his tracks or, I should say, those of his children. Because of his concern for his children and their relationship with God, Job did this on a regular basis.

One day the angels gave the Lord an update of their activity on the earth. It so happened that on this day, Satan came with them. The Lord asked Satan, "What have you been up to?" "Oh, nothing. I have been merely walking around the earth checking things out," he replied. The Lord asked Satan, "In all of your travels have you ever seen such a person as my friend Job? He is an honest, loyal, and decent man, always doing the right thing." Satan quickly responded by saying, "Why do you think he is such a good person? Do you think that he is doing what he is doing out of devotion and the goodness of his heart? Not on your life. No one has been so well-off and catered to like Job. He has the best of everything. He has been so cared for that he hasn't a need for anything in the world. You have protected him and his family from harm. You have made his possessions secure — so that he can't lose. The truth is that if you took all of this security and all of these possessions away from him — he would curse you to your face. That's for sure! No doubt about it!"

God replied, "We'll see about that. Go ahead and do to him all you want, but don't hurt him." What God is saying is — you can go so far and no further. Having gained access to Job's possessions, Satan left the presence of the Lord scheming in his mind what he might do to Job. He was going to take advantage of his opportunity.

One day a messenger came running in from the range in a state of panic. He said to Job, "While the oxen were plowing and the donkeys were feeding in the field next to them, the Sabeans attacked us. With their swords they killed all of the servants and carried all the animals away. I am the only survivor and I ran as quickly as I could to tell you what happened." Even before the servant could finish his account another messenger arrived informing Job that a ferocious thunderstorm with great bolts of lightning had struck the sheep and the shepherds killing all of them and that he was the only one who survived. No sooner had he finished than another messenger arrived to inform Job that Chaldeans had swept down from hills on three sides engulfing the camels and their drivers. With their swords they killed the drivers and carried off all the camels. The messenger told Job, "I am the only survivor." Before

Job could get his thoughts together or register what was happening to him in this whirlwind of events, another messenger arrived informing Job that his children were having a party at his oldest son's home when a tornado struck without warning totally destroying the house. All of his children were killed. "I am the only one that survived and I ran to tell you what happened."

Job was stunned. He was numb. He knelt on the ground. He was saying to himself, "What on earth has happened to me?" He knelt for a long period of time — saying nothing. His head bowed and his shoulders stooped appearing like a man who had been beaten senseless with a whip. Finally after a long silence he struggled to his feet. He ripped his robe, shaved his head, fell to the ground and worshiped. In a somber, subdued voice he said: "Naked I came from my mother's womb, naked shall I return there; the Lord gave and the Lord has taken away, blessed be the name of the Lord" (1:21).

At no time in all that had happened did Job sin or blame God for his misfortune.

Once again on the fringe of creation God met with the angels so they might give an account of their activity on earth, and Satan was again with them. God spoke directly to Satan by asking him, "What have you been up to?" "I have been traveling throughout the earth checking things out," he replied.

God asked Satan again, "What do you think of my man Job? Just like I said, he is unique; there is no one quite like him. He is honest and trustworthy, and he's still loyal to me and hates evil. He is still a man of integrity even though you tried to destroy him. Like I said, there is no one quite like Job on earth."

Then Satan challenged God. "Anyone would be loyal to you to save his life. They would be a fool to do otherwise. If Job were to lose his health and possibly his life, the truth is, he would curse you to your face." God replied, "We shall see. Go ahead. He is in your hands. Do to him whatever you please, but I insist, don't kill him." So Satan left God's presence anxious to carry out his scheme against Job.

Satan inflicted Job with painful ulcers and scabs all over his body. The itching was so unbearable that he took pieces of broken pottery to scrape himself. He could not get any respite from his pain, and he finally went and sat on a rubbish pile amid the ashes seeking relief.

In his misery and pain his wife came to him and said, "After all that has happened to you are you going to continue in this foolish integrity? If you had any wit about you you would curse God and die." Slowly but deliberately Job responded, "Woman, you are foolish to speak like that. We need to take the good days that God has given to us, along with the bad."

I have always had appreciation for Leslie Wheatherhead's insightful statement suggesting that after we have had a painful human experience we ought to get from that experience everything it has to teach us, because we have paid such a high price for the wisdom it seeks to impart. Job has just had a very painful experience, beyond anything most of us could imagine. What was his immediate response? Simply, that we need to take the good days along with the bad. It is a remarkable response for a man who has lost so much. This is remarkable because this is not what you would expect. Many would respond with anger and resentment demanding an explanation from God. "Why? Why me and why mine? How could God permit such a thing to happen? Haven't I tried to live a good life?" Because of one's overwhelming loss and pain there is no thought that anything good or meaningful could ever come from such a experience. A good many people look at human suffering and say, "Don't talk to me about God!"

Job's statement is remarkable. He was willing to take the good with the bad, but the bad seemed so much more than the good. He lost everything — his children, his possessions, it was all gone. What good is left? But Job is saying goodness is not to be calculated in things. Is there a meaning to faith beyond possessions and family? George Mattheson was engaged to a young woman whom he deeply loved, and they planned to be married. In the meantime, Mattheson lost his eyesight — he became totally sightless. His fiance told him that she could not marry him. She could not marry a sightless man. The marriage was asking more from her than she could give and she left him. He was devastated. Amid his brokenness and loneliness he sat down at the piano and wrote the hymn

"O Love That Will Not Let Me Go." Listen to the words of the first verse,

> *O Love that will not let me go,*
> *I rest my weary soul in thee.*
> *I give thee back the life I owe,*
> *that in thine ocean depths its flow may richer,*
> *fuller be.*

He experienced a love that let him go, but he also experienced a greater love, regardless of whatever happened to him, that would never let him go. In the darkest moment of his life he made his greatest discovery.

Job sat on the ash pile contemplating everything that had happened to him. All hell had broken out against him. Even his wife had let him down. Because of her unutterable loss she believed that she could no longer bear life where all visible tokens of God's presence and favor were gone. She cried out to her husband in this impossible horror: "Curse God and die!"

In the darkest moment of his life he made a great discovery — life is a combination of good and evil, blessing and pain, moments of ecstasy and agony, bad days and good days. Job had just experienced some very bad days that brought indescribable horror and pain. Remarkably, he did not lose sight of goodness. He talked about "the good days from God." He was still able to talk about those moments of goodness amid his loss and pain. He saw this goodness as something that came to his life from God. Because of this goodness he did not do what his wife admonished him to do. He did not curse God. Life was a combination of goodness and evil, blessing and pain, but because of the goodness from God, Job felt that life was infinitely worthwhile.

I am certain that Job must have said to himself what most people say in a moment like that: *Where is God?* How often I have been asked that question. That question has a sense of abandonment. The person asking the question feels that God is distant. Recently a SwissAire jetliner bound for Geneva crashed off the coast of Nova Scotia killing all 220 people aboard. As I watched the televsion coverage of the crash, I saw family members standing on the rocky shore line of Peggy's Cove staring out through the fog toward where the plane had gone down. As they stood silently looking out over the water I imagined that in their minds were the words, "Where is God now?" There is only one answer to that question. God is where God has always been — loving, sustaining, and caring for his own.

Proper 23 • Pentecost 21 • Ordinary Time 28

# Making Our Feelings Known

*Job 23:1-9, 16-17*

---

**In our text** Job makes his lament to God loud and clear, "Today also my complaint is bitter." The word *bitter* seems to carry the feeling of defiance in the wake of grievance and complaint. Job earlier has spoken of the bitterness of his soul:

> *Therefore I will not restrain my mouth;*
> *I will speak in the anguish of my spirit;*
> *I will complain in the bitterness of my soul.* (7:11)
>
> *I loathe my life;*
> *I will give free utterance to my complaint.* (10:1)

Here Job is correlating his own bitter defiance with the unrelenting pressure of God's hand upon his life. Job insists on seeking a resolution for his complaint not through the traditional religious practices of prayer and lament (as in the Psalms), but through a legal hearing, because he feels that he has a case against God. But Job is confronted with a dilemma: he does not know how to find his way into God's presence.[1] Previously, Job felt that he was blocked in his desire to have a hearing with God by God's overwhelming power.

> *For he is not a mortal, as I am, that I might answer him,*
> *that we could come to trial together.*
> *There is no umpire between us, who might lay his hand on us both.*

> *If he would take his rod away from me,*
> *then I would speak without fear of him,*
> *for I know I am not what I am thought to be.* (9:32-35)

> *Only grant two things to me,*
> *then I will not hide myself from your face.*
> *Withdraw your hand far from me,*
> *and do not let dread of you terrify me.* (13:20-21)

Then Job senses God's dread.

> *Would he contend with me in the*
> *greatness of his power?*
> *No, but he would give heed to me.*

His desire for trial is blocked by God's elusiveness.

> *If I go forward, he is not there;*
> *or backward, I cannot perceive him;*
> *on the left he hides me, and I cannot behold him;*
> *I turn to the right, but I cannot see him.*

Each of these half lines ends by reiterating the crucial point: "He is not there," "I cannot not perceive him," "I cannot see him," "I cannot glimpse him." Job's frustrated search for God is such a contrast to Psalm 139. Even though he cannot perceive God, he senses that God perceives him: "But he knows the way I take" (v. 10a). He now has the feeling that God's knowledge of him will ensure his vindication: "when he has tested me I shall come out like gold" ( v. 10b).

One of the remarkable things regarding the Scriptures is how they give feeling to the personal lament of men and women. At no time does the Bible hide such feelings. The anger, the frustration, and the disappointment that people feel in regard to God's apparent absence from human life along with the feelings of a lack of justice and fair play on God's part is all played out in the Scriptures for all to see and hear. Job is permitted to lay it all out before

God for all to see. These feelings are still with us today, if not more so.

We identify with Job and the lament of the other Old Testament writers because they express our own feelings. Life today is marked by what Walter Brueggemann calls, "disequilibrium, incoherence, and unrelieved assymetry."[2] It is clear that a church or a Christian who goes on singing "happy songs" in the face of such glaring disorientation is very different from what the Bible itself portrays, particularly in Job. The reason for the lack of lament, as seen in our text, stems from the thought that the acknowledgment of such negativity is somehow an act of unfaith, suggesting that God has lost control. Some would see such statements of unfaith or failure, whereas the biblical laments are to be seen as acts of *bold faith*. Brueggemann points out that

> *it is an act of bold faith on the one hand, because it insists that the world must be experienced as it really is and not in some pretended way. On the one hand, it is bold because it insists that all such experiences of disorder are a proper subject for discourse with God. There is nothing out of bounds, nothing precluded or inappropriate. Everything properly belongs to this conversation of the heart. To withhold parts of life from that conversation is in fact to withhold part of life from the sovereignty of God.* [3]

The frank language of Job taking God to task and seeking to have a trial before God so that he can lay his feelings bare is something the church and the Christian have intuitively avoided. The reason for such avoidance of speech as seen in Job and other biblical writers is that it leads one into the dangerous acknowledgment of how life really is. Through such speech Job leads us into the presence of God where everything is not polite and civil. As Brueggemann suggests, they cause us to think unthinkable thoughts and to utter the unutterable to the surprise of many. But at no time did God reprimand Job for making his feelings known. Notice that Job brings his case directly to God. What he so earnestly and honestly feels in his heart is brought to speech, and everything that is brought to speech is directed to God. In Job's speech nothing is out of bounds, nothing is considered as inappropriate. The deep feelings of his heart are expressed to God, who is the final reference for all of life. For both Job and ourselves, honest confession is a catharsis cleansing the heart, and such honest confession produces transformation. Every biblical writer who, in the midst of doubt and despair, makes his feelings known to God breaks forth into a new discovery of faith. (An exception would be Psalm 88).

The Book of Job after all is not a book on suffering, but rather one of faith. Job has had a devastating experience losing all of his possessions and his family. What makes this so difficult for Job is that it does not fit his understanding of God. The problem for Job in all of this is that it has happened as though there was no God, and if there was a God, God did not care one whit for justice. This is Job's problem.

But this is also our problem. Richard Rubenstein, the outstanding Jewish theologian, said, "God died at Auschwitz." For many God seemed to die in the midst of their personal tragedy and suffering. So much suffering appears senseless, meaningless, unexplainable, and causes many to express their personal lament and anguish by calling into question the goodness, as well as the very existence of God. Many have cried out as Job, "Oh, that I knew where I might find him" (v. 3).

The storms of life come to us as they came to Job. We learn what he learned: we cannot rely on our friends; we cannot rely on our wealth; we cannot rely on our family. We can only and ultimately do as Job did: cast ourselves completely on God, who cradles us in the bosom of God's love and grace bringing assurance that God is totally in control.

---

1. Carol Newson, "Job," *New Interpreter's Bible*, Vol. 4, p. 508.

2. Walter Brueggemann, *Message of the Psalms*, p. 53.

3. *Ibid.*, p. 52.

*Proper 24  •  Pentecost 22  •  Ordinary Time 29*

## Out Of The Whirlwind

*Job 38:1-7 (34-41)*

---

**God answers** Job out of the whirlwind. There is no better word to explain what has taken place in Job's life than a whirlwind. Look at the events that have transpired in his life: all his children are dead; his home and business are lost; he lost his health, and his body is disfigured with open sores. It all happened in rapid-fire succession — just like a whirlwind. Out of the whirlwind Job asks God, "Why?" He is so despondent that he wishes he was dead. "Let the day perish wherein I was born."

Job reveals to us how difficult and dangerous it can become trying to answer the questions regarding human suffering. But he is not alone. His three lifelong friends, Eliphaz, Bildad, and Zophar, come to share with Job their feelings regarding his calamity. Like us, as they approached their forlorn friend, they wondered what on earth they were going to say. Like us, they approached in a timid, uncertain, and tentative manner. Under their breath they were saying, "Thank God it isn't me." For seven days they sat in silence. They looked with disbelief at the sight before them. As is often the case, in the face of such tragedy they did not know what to say. In their silence they were possibly focusing on their own lives, contemplating what they would do if such events ever happened to them, and what behavior they would have to follow to prevent it from ever happening to them. It took them seven days to figure out what to say, and as it happens many times in such a situation, they said the wrong things.

Eliphaz finally breaks the silence. He proceeds to tell Job what happened, why it happened, and what to do about it. Here is Job sitting on the ash pile in misery listening to his friend say to him, "Now Job, think, who do you know that was innocent who ever perished? You appear to be perishing. Now let's try and figure out what you have done to deserve this." Eliphaz was trying to reason logically with Job at a time when Job was operating not on a "thinking" but on a "feeling" level. Logic, reason, and argument are not what Job needed. Then his second friend, Bildad, begins his speech by saying, "Are you suggesting that God is unjust? If you were pure and upright, God would answer you with prosperity." Job's third friend, Zophar, picks up the conversation by chiding Job, "How dare you ask such question of God? Why would God take the trouble to explain himself to a liar like you?" The questions asked of Job were as painful as his suffering. Yet, it sounds so familiar. Our answers are just as poor and painful when we say to a friend in pain, "It is just God's will. You will have to accept it." "God never puts on anyone more than he or she can bear." "If you had enough faith you could get out of this mess." "I know how you feel." "AIDS, after all, is their own fault." These statements are cruel and harsh. William Willimon has suggested that "most of us, realizing the inadequacy of our theology of chaos have learned to mutter the more sophisticated, 'Well, er, uh, we'll be thinking about you.'"

In his book, *The Spiritual Life*, Robert Cole interviews little Margarita whose life is characterized by the brutal hillside favela in Rio.

> When I look at Jesus up there (she points towards the well-known "Christ of the Andes" statue whose arms are outstretched over Rio), I wonder what He's thinking. He can see all of us, and He must have an opinion. I try to walk with Him ... He is all that I have, Mama still works as a maid in Copocabana, even though she coughs and bleeds. A lot of times I asked Him why He does things like this. (She waves her hand in the arc, encompassing the squalid favela). He must see what we see ... Mother used to tell us we'll go to heaven, because we are poor. I used to believe her ... She just says that — it is a way of shutting us all up when we're

*hungry! Now, when I hear her say it, I look up at Him and I ask Him: What do you say Jesus? Do you believe her? Do you believe the priest who says the same thing? Do you notice the big car he drives and do you notice that big house he has? ... What do you think of him? ... I shouldn't blame Jesus! I do, though, sometimes. He's right there — the statue keeps reminding me of Him ... and I'm either upset with Him or I'm praying for Him to tell me why the world is like it is.* (p. 91)

Margarita's plight is much like that of Job. His friends were telling him all of these same old trite Sunday school cliches: God helps those who help themselves; obey God and you will be blessed; this is all for your good; break God's rules and God will break you. For them religion is nice, stable, neat, and predictable. But Job is relentless in his desire to have answers. He wants to know: Who is to blame? Why did this happen to me? Is the Lord unjust or fair? Young Margarita looks up at the stone statue over the squalor of her community and demands an answer. Job defiantly tells God, "I'll see you in court!"

Now, in chapter 38 God arrives on the scene. Out of the whirlwind God answers Job. And what a God confronts Job! Job was not prepared for this. After all Job's accusations and his threatening to take God to court — God arrives on the scene and without mincing words declares, "Gird up your loins like a man." In other words God says to Job, "Stand up before me like a man because I have something to tell you. Who is this one that dares to speak? Where were you when I laid the foundations of the earth. Are you the one that made the sun to rise? Who are you?"

For those of us who think that our God is docile and soft spoken, here is God taking on Job with bombastic, whirlwind rhetoric. When God answers, God answers with questions, insolent questions: Where were you? Who are you? What have you done? Willimon suggests what God is really saying to Job is, "Shut up and listen to me." God assures Job that the story of his life is not over. God is saying, "It is not over until I say it is over." If Job's forced resignation and quiet capitulation is the end, then he is really in trouble. If God does not answer Job's questions then any answer he comes up with, no matter how trite or nihilistic, would appear as good as any. Fortunately, this is not the end of the story. God continues to speak.

God reminds Job that it is God who is the master architect and builder and Job had no part in it. What stands out in these verses is the manner in which God is allowing Job to discover how ridiculous his supposed "wisdom" is. One scholar suggests that the story is like that of a parent who lovingly puts down a child's unwarranted rebellion, not because the child has offended the parent or because the parent's dignity is at stake, but rather because it is important for the child, before any conversation can continue, to acknowledge the parent's authority and the reason for it. So God speaks firmly and directly to Job that Job has no misunderstanding of God's purpose. Throughout the earlier chapters of Job, Job has demanded an answer from God regarding the events of his life. Now he has God's response through chapters 38-41. Remarkably through God's speech the focus slowly turns to God's loving care for all of creation — something that Job finds difficult to do.

No matter how unfair or misguided Job's argument may be, God answers him out of the whirlwind. God never called Job foolish, insolent, or unfair in his arguments. God allowed him to make his case against God and then God answers. Out of the whirlwind of Job's life God comes to him. God comes to him where he is. Job discovers that his story is to be seen in light of God's bigger story. The bigger story is that God came to Israel in the midst of the whirlwind. It was God who came to them in slavery. It was God who observed the misery of his people in Egypt. It was God who heard their cries for relief from their slave masters. It was God who brought them out from the bondage of the Egyptians to a good and broad land, a land flowing with milk and honey. God came to the Israelites in the midst of the whirlwind. God came to them in the midst of their slavery, in their struggle for freedom, at the time of the ruthlessness of Pharaoh. When they needed direction it was God who led them by a cloud during the day and a pillar of fire by night. When they were hungry it was God who fed them with manna from heaven. When they were thirsty it was God who provided water from the rock. Job needed to see his story in relation to this bigger story. If God did that for Israel, God could do the same for Job. If God spoke to Israel in the midst of the whirlwind, God could also speak to Job in the midst of his whirlwind. That is exactly what God did. The word for us today is that God comes to us in the midst of the whirlwind. From this story of Job we learn that God is a loving God. God is an infinitely caring God. God is a sustaining and forgiving God. God comes to us in the midst of our whirlwind. Another thing we notice in this story of Job is that God has a wonderful sense of humor. Job 38-41 is a remarkable discourse where God's classic reply to Job puts him in his place, firmly, absolutely, but with infinite love and compassion. One cannot help but read this discourse with a smile. For a long period of time Job takes God to task for his plight, and then calmly and with assurance God says to Job, "Let me tell you who I am." In the midst of the whirlwind Job discovers who God is.

God comes to us in the midst of the whirlwind. It may be that just when everything is going great and it appears that God is smiling on your life the unexpected happens. It may have been the result of a devastating diagnosis that leads to the deterioration of your health; the loss of your job; the yielding to temptation that compromises your relationship with your spouse or children bringing a sense of shame and loss. It may be the breaking of a relationship by divorce or death and for the first time you are alone. It strikes with the force of a whirlwind and knocks your breath out, causing confusion and fear. What is one to do? We do what Job did. We listen to our friends who give us pious reasons for our misfortune, discovering in their answers not comfort, but more pain and confusion. That's when we need to relate our story to the bigger story of God's love for us in Jesus Christ. We need to know that God is a God who comes to us in the midst of the whirlwind, in the midst of the storm, in the midst of the pain and lostness. The bigger picture is that God comes to us where we are. Isn't that the message of the Bible? Isn't that the message of the incarnation? God comes to us in Christ right where we are. God does not ask us to clean ourselves up and come to God. This is the very thing we cannot do. God in Christ comes to us where we, at our level, and looks us squarely in the eye, asking, "Where does it hurt and how can I help?"

The Lord answered Job out of the whirlwind — God will do the same for you.

Proper 25 • Pentecost 23 • Ordinary Time 30

# Confession

*Job 42:1-6, 10-17*

---

**Job got what** he wanted. He got a chance to present his case before God and to hear God's response. After hearing God's reply to him, he confesses that he said things that he really did not understand. There were things about God, creation, and human life that were just too wonderful for him, things that he did not know. His accusation before God now seemed to him to be ludicrous and unwarranted.

But at no time did God ever chastise him for speaking his mind. It was those moments of desertion and abandonment and the absence of God's presence that most of his hearers and readers identify with Job. This is the universal feeling of those who have walked the path of faith. Who has not felt at some time in life forsaken by God? How many times have you prayed and felt, saw, and sensed nothing? There have been those times when heaven seems like brass and God has turned a deaf ear. We do everything we can do. We pray. We attend church. We get involved in mission programs. We read the scriptures and pray daily, but to no avail. No matter how hard we practice all of these Christian disciplines, it all appears meaningless. God seems hidden. In those moments we need to gain some sense of perspective. It would be foolish for us to think this experience is uniquely ours, that we are the only ones who experience this desert of the soul. To think such would reveal our ignorance and how little we know of our Christian faith. We must not forget how Moses waited year after year in silence for God to deliver his people. Think of those Psalms of lament. Go back and read Psalms 13, 74, and especially 88 — the Psalms that Walter Brueggemann calls the "Psalms of disorientation." These biblical laments allow us to pray our conflicts, frustrations, and contradictions. Go back and read about Elijah, Jeremiah, and above all Habakkuk and Jesus in Gethsemane. This will be encouraging to you as you realize that with all of your frustration and anxiety you are in good company. Let us remember that as we speak about the absence of God, it is not a true absence, but a *sense* of God's absence. Theologically, God is always with us, but there are those moments that we are not conscious of God's presence. It is during those moments that we need to hold steady and remember what we have known of God in the past, until the clouds lift and the sun shines again. Richard Foster suggests:

> *Through all of this, paradoxically, God is purifying our fatih by threatening to destroy it. We are led to a profound and holy distrust of all superficial drives and human strivings. We know more deeply than ever before our capacity for infinite self-deception. Slowly we are being taken off of vain securities and false allegiances. Our trust in all exterior and interior results is being shattered so that we can learn faith in God alone. Through our barrenness of soul God is producing detachment, humility, patience and perseverance.*[1]

In this final chapter Job responds to God's address to him. Job repents. He recognizes himself for what he is. He confesses that he made accusations falsely: "Therefore I have uttered what I did not understand." He apologizes for his arrogance and self-presupposing regarding both his friends and God. Now Job is able to do something he has found difficult to do: he accepts God's power and wisdom. He ends up where his friends said he would end up, recognizing that God is all-powerful and all-knowing and all Job can do is accept what is happening to him and live with it. But Job's confession includes the words, "I heard of you by the hearing of the ear, but now my eye sees you." He admits that he now has a personal knowledge of God that he never before had. He confesses that his knowledge of God has been secondhand. He learned of God from the community and its members who happened to inform him about God. In verse 6, Job feels bad and despises himself for his lack of understanding of God and "repents in dust and ashes."

Job's greatest discovery in this encounter is his personal experience of God and the understanding that he can continue to question God and God will answer. Job's repentance is not as his friends thought it should be, an annihilation of himself, a total submission which reduces him to a despondent man on an ash pile. But now Job knows about a God who responds. Now he knows that he will always belong to God. Whatever, whenever, wherever, however things may transpire in Job's life, he will continue to question and have honest dialogue with God. The difference now is his awareness that God is in control. This is the "joyful and happy ending" of the Book of Job.

In this entire experience Job has learned to trust God. Prior to his trusting, things appeared out of control in his life. Confusion and chaos abounded. The result of his trust was his discovery that God, after all, is in control and that life does have a center, a whole, and above all meaning. Job discovered that God did not need to be defended, as suggested by his friends who felt it was their responsibility to intervene and defend God in light of Job's plight. This seems to be a chronic problem within the church. There are those people who are always coming up with methods and gimmicks, acting as if the power of the gospel depended on them. Perhaps the reason that this book has been so valuable for so many people for such a long period of time is the very fact that "it is in the Bible," giving us permission to challenge and question God when our suffering compels us to do so. This very questioning, the honest expression of our doubts and uncertainties, is what builds trust.

The struggle in Job's life is an inspiration to all of us. Who hasn't struggled over the whereabouts of God's presence in human life? How many times have you heard the question, "How can a good God allow such suffering in the world?" Job's lack of trust was a result of his uncertainty about the character of God. After all, Satan was given permission by God to take away Job's family, his business, and his health. Was God playing a cruel joke on Job? Because he was unable to find a purpose or a reason for his suffering, he lays the blame on God. Job confesses, "Today also my complaint is bitter; his hand is heavy despite my groaning" (23:2). Job felt that God acted unjustly toward him. How is he going to trust such a God?

Here is where the change takes place. The turning point in Job's life is found in 42:5: *"I had heard of you by the hearing of the ear, but now my eye sees you."* Up to this point Job has only known about God by what he had heard from others. His faith was secondhand. Job listened to his friends and his knowledge of God came from them. His friends presented God as a mere object, when in reality God is a living, caring, personal, loving God. When Job declared, "But now my eye sees you," his own personal awareness of God frees him from the narrow, provincial God of his friends. His personal experience of God has liberated him from the confining understanding of God that had so characterized his earlier life. This is the turning point in Job's life. He turns from a secondhand knowledge of God to a personal encounter with God. What had been merely abstract and mental accent was transformed into personal experience and awareness. What had been distant and ambiguous was now close and real. What had been detached and remote was now genuine loving concern. The transcendent and inaccessible was now lovingly and graciously immanent.

How many times have I heard the same story. A person grows up in the church, attends Sunday school and worship services for years, works his fingers to the bone on church projects, and serves faithfully on committees. But like Job, his knowledge of God is secondhand. Then through some remarkable experience he discovers that he has no personal experience of God. His religion has been perfunctory. It has been merely part of his respectability along with being a good citizen. Church membership was on the same level as being a member of the Kiwanis and the Lions Club. Then one day, possibly at a church retreat, the person discovers that people were witnessing to a reality of faith that he has never possessed or known. Through the prayers of his friends his entire life changes. The things that were so important in his life are no longer important. Things that were considered to be unimportant and secondary became primary. The person is able to say with Job, "I heard of you by the hearing of the ear, but now my eye sees you."

Job confesses, "But now my eye sees you." Job states that he now perceives God in a way that transforms his understanding of himself and his situation. "Seeing" involves more than just having one's eyes open. Not only does it involve seeing God differently, but when we see God differently we also see others and our world differently. One becomes conscious of the needs of others. A new vision of God brings into focus the injustice in the lives of others. A new vision of God brings to us a new awareness of the needs of others. What is out of sight many times is out of mind: the homeless, shelters for abused women and children, homes for the poor, food for the hungry, support for those who suffer through the violation of their human and civil rights, and support of AIDS coalitions. But we gain new vision and understanding for them as the result of a new awareness of God. It seems that the closer one is drawn to God through worship and prayer, the closer one is drawn to the aliens of our culture, the many people clustered at the margins of society, and those who live on the fringes of the law. This new vision of God was a turning point in Job's life. He acquired a new understanding of his life and the world around him. It can do the same for us — to see God and others as we have never seen them before.

---

1. Richard Foster, *Prayer*, p. 29.

*Proper 26 • Pentecost 24 • Ordinary Time 31*

# The Tale Of Three Women

*Ruth 1:1-18*

---

**Ruth, what a** remarkable book. Here is an interesting portrayal of three women — Naomi, Orpah, and Ruth. Against the brutal setting of a famine in Judah, Elimelech flees from Judah with his wife Naomi and their two sons to the country of Moab in search of food. After their arrival in Moab Elimelech dies leaving his wife Naomi alone with her two sons Mahlon and Chilion. The two sons marry Moabite women, Naomi and Ruth. Ten years later the husbands of Ruth and Naomi die leaving all three woman widowed. Naomi decides to return to Judah and her two daughters-in-law travel with her. On her journey to her homeland Naomi insists that Orpah and Ruth should return to Moab. She urges them, "Go back each of you to your mother's house and may the Lord deal kindly with you as you have dealt with me." But the women answer, "No, we will return with you to your people." Naomi insists that they return to Moab. After giving her mother-in-law's words serious consideration, Orpah kisses her mother-in-law goodbye and returns to Moab, but Ruth remains and "clings" to Naomi. Then we have these memorable words of Ruth:

> *Do not press me to leave you*
> *Or to turn back from following you!*
> *Where you go, I will go;*
> *   Where you lodge I will lodge;*
> *Your people shall be my people,*
> *   And your God my God.*

*Where you die, I will die —*
*there I will be buried.*
*May the Lord do thus and so to me,*
*and more as well.* (vv. 16-17)

When Naomi sees that Ruth has decided to stay with her, she never says another word to her about returning to Moab, but the two women travel to Judah together.

**Naomi**

The story takes place during the time of the judges in Israel. According to the last verse of the book of Judges, it was a time of ineffectual political leadership: "All the people did what was right in their own eyes." Not only was there political instability, but there was economic disaster as well, "there was famine in the land." Famine in the ancient near East meant bloated bellies of little children, old people dying in the streets, people wandering aimlessly begging for food. Elimelech and his wife pack up all of their earthly possessions and head for Moab, because he had heard that things were better there. Why would anyone want to travel to Moab? It is a rough, out-of-the-way sort of place. Back in Genesis after Abraham and Lot departed company and after Lot's wife was turned into a pillar of salt, Lot was on his own, so he went up and lived in a cave with his two daughters. His daughters were unmarried. Since they were getting old they felt that their chances of marriage were very slim. They proceeded to get their father drunk, and while he was drunk they went in to him and nine months later they each had a son by their father. One of the sons was Moab, who became the father of the Moabites (Genesis 19:37). Life in Moab was rough-and-tumble, to say the least. One had to be really desperate for food to move his family there. No sooner had they arrived than the worst possible thing happened: Naomi's husband dies and she is now a single parent in a brutal, harsh land with the responsibility of raising two teenage sons.

Kathleen A. Robertson Farmer, in her commentary on Ruth, points out that Naomi in chapter one comes across as an unattractive character. Although her name means "sweetness," she does not come across as sweet. After the death of her husband and sons she blames God for the emptiness she feels. She feels the loss of her family is the result of divine judgment. She suggests that possibly God is responsible for their deaths. Naomi feels that she left Judah with a husband, two sons, and a promising future, and because of the Lord's doing she is returning empty-handed. But she has a right to be bitter and angry — after all she has lost her husband and sons. Who wouldn't feel bitter? Anger would be the most logical initial response to such a catastrophe. Anyone who has experienced what Naomi experienced will confess that their first response was one of bitterness and anger. Not only is it logical and understandable, but healthy. Anger is part of the healing process. Anger in the face of such tragedy is not only expressed but needs to be worked and prayed through. It is part of both the grieving and the healing processes. God does not condemn anyone for expressing anger and bitterness in the face of tragedy — consider Job, the Psalms, and Habakkuk.

This grieving, bitter widow accomplished something that all of us would hope to accomplish. She influenced someone to choose to follow her God. Naomi became the instrument of Ruth's choice to make Naomi's God her God. This did not come about by Naomi putting on a "happy face," but by being her true self. Here is hope for us, as weak and faulty as we may be. God can use us, as God used Naomi in the midst of her bitterness and grief, to accomplish no small part in the work of God in the world.

**Orpah**

Naomi pleaded with her daughters-in-law to go back to their mothers' houses in Moab. She pleaded with the Lord to deal as kindly with them as they had dealt with her and that they might find security in their husbands' families. Noami wept as she kissed each of them. Both Orpah and Ruth insisted, "No, we will return with you to your people." Naomi pleaded with them to return to their homeland. She said she was too old to bear sons who could become their husbands. She tried to reason with them by stating, "Should I have a husband tonight and bear sons, would you then wait until they were grown?" She insisted that they turn back. Orpah kisses her mother-in-law goodbye and returns. Her leave-taking is expressed in the briefest possible manner. It has been suggested that Orpah functions as a foil for Ruth, who acts in the opposite manner. Orpah leaves, but Ruth "clings" to Naomi. Orpah never speaks in the entire narrative, whereas Ruth makes a lengthy speech dismissing all of Naomi's arguments on why she should return as irrelevant.

Orpah does everything society and the authority figures in her life would expect her to do. She obeys her mother-in-law and returns to her people in Moab, although she weeps as she goes. It is interesting that rabbinic legends state that the four giant warriors mentioned in 2 Samuel 21:22 were Orpah's sons, but in fact she vanishes from the official biblical narrative. Kathleen Robertson Farmer points out that Orpah is the model of obedient womanhood and that the Lord may have eventually dealt kindly with her as she had dealt kindly with Naomi and Ruth. Farmer points out that no one elected to tell her story. "In a similar way, many modern women who have chosen traditional lifestyles, living lives of obedience to the expectations of society or the authority figures in their lives, may feel that no one is interested in telling their stories."[2] Bonnie Miller McLemore states: "Orpah's journey home helps us to reconsider the silent and silenced among us, those who stand both on the threshold of the woman's movement and on the threshold of traditional beliefs and practices."[3] It has been pointed out that the biblical narrator does not condemn Orpah, nor should we. The Orpahs and the Ruths among us should be remembered and celebrated.

### Ruth

Naomi declares to Ruth, "Look, your sister-in-law is going back to her people and her gods. Go back with her." But Ruth replies: "Don't urge me to leave you or to turn back from you. Where you go I will go, where you stay I will stay. Your people will be my people and your God my God." Naomi has taken a commonsense approach as she tries to reason with Ruth. Why would she want to travel with an old, barren woman to a strange and foreign land?

Naomi can see no way that Ruth could benefit from her association with her. There is no good reason why Ruth should "cling" to her mother-in-law. But Ruth's actions are those of love and loyalty rather than reason or logic. When Noami realizes that it is futile to reason with her daughter-in-law, she then is silent and does not speak to her. The story does not tell us the reason for Naomi's silence. Was it because she was overwhelmed by Ruth's devotion to her, or was she angry?

This story seems strange to us. Why would anybody want to limit his or her options by becoming unnecessarily tied down by the messy complications of other people? The story of Ruth and Naomi is one of two women who in a sense are strangers coming from two different parts of the world, yet they are bound together in the midst of a hostile world. This is a story of relationships, of family. To be in any family is to venture forth like Ruth and Naomi, without guarantees for the future, but, even in the worst of futures, it is more hopeful and bearable when we bear it with one another. God was about to work out a remarkable future for Ruth. She wasn't sure what it all meant, but she had the feeling that her life was to have significance and meaning, if she was faithful and loyal, although things appeared mysterious. At this point in her life she is akin to Mary, the mother of Jesus. Mary knew that something important and significant was about to take place, but she was not certain what it all meant. For Mary, her future too was wrapped in mystery and awe. The secret is if we just stick together, trust God through the thick and thin, God will use such faithfulness and fidelity to reveal God's purpose and bless others.

---

1. Kathleen A. Robertson Farmer, "Ruth," in *New Interpreter's Bible, Volume 2* (Abingdon Press, 1998).

2. *Ibid.*, p. 906.

3. Bonnie Miller McLemore, *Christian Century*, April 17, 1991, p. 430.

*Proper 27* • *Pentecost 25* • *Ordinary Time 32*

# Expanding The Boundaries

*Ruth 3:1-5; 4:13-17*

---

**The Book of** Ruth is a family story. It is an old story, possibly over three thousand years old. It is a story about a family in trouble. Let me briefly summarize the story. Elimelech flees with his wife and two sons from the famine in Israel and heads for Moab because they heard that things were better there. In desperation they move to Moab, an out-of-the-way sort of place. You would have to be desperate, really hungry to move your family to Moab. Soon after their arrival Naomi's husband dies and she is left with two sons in a foreign land. Her sons, Mahon and Chilion, took Moabite wives, Orpah and Ruth. Ten years after their arrival in Moab Naomi's sons die. She again is in a desperate situation, but this time she has no one to fall back on. She is alone with her two daughters-in-law.

Naomi feels like she has no choice but to return to Bethlehem. She says to her two daughters-in-law, "I am going back home to Bethlehem, back to my people, back to my roots. I am a single woman with no marketable skills, no hope of ever marrying again, no future. You need to go back to Moab and your people. You should not be hanging around an old lady like me. Go back to your people where you belong. Go to your people where there is some hope for you. It is hopeless if you follow me to Bethlehem. You are Moabites not Israelites." Orpah leaves and returns to Moab, but Ruth "clings" to Naomi. In one of the most beloved speeches in the Bible she says to Naomi, "Entreat me not to leave you or to return from following you, for where you go I will go. Where you lodge I will lodge. Your people will be my people and your God will be my God." They leave together for Israel. William Willimon reminds us, "To be in any family is to venture forth like Naomi and Ruth, without guarantees for the future, with only the confidence that the future, even the worst of futures, is bearable when we bear it with one another."

The most remarkable part of this story is yet to be told. Ruth finally gets to Israel, thanks to Naomi. Ruth, by a strange set of circumstances, meets a man named Boaz. Ruth marries Boaz and they have a son. The son's name is Obed, and lo and behold, this son born of a non-Israelite Moab woman is to become the grandfather of King David of Israel. Thus, Ruth, a foreign, Moabite woman, through the twisting and turning of providence, is in the blood line, the genealogy, leading up to the birth of Jesus in Bethlehem.

In this story we discover how, in all of the mundane struggles of ordinary day-to-day life, Ruth, the Moabite, plays an important role in keeping the promise and the covenant of God to Israel alive, thus bringing it to eventual fruition. Ruth, through her loyalty and faithfulness to Naomi, finds a surprisingly open future. Is God active in the ordinary, mundane everyday happening? Undoubtedly, the writer wants us to ask ourselves this question as we encounter the story of Ruth.

We discover in the genealogy in Matthew 1:5-6 "that Obed, Ruth's son, is an ancestor of King David who is an ancestor of King Jesus." Is there any significance to Ruth's name being included in Matthew's genealogy? Bible scholars believe there is great significance to be found in the inclusion of Ruth's name. It has been pointed out that the most surprising thing about Matthew's genealogy is that it should even contain the names of women. Women never appeared in Jewish genealogies. Why should they? Women had no rights; they were at the disposal of their husbands. Women were not regarded as persons but possessions. In the morning prayers it was common for a Jewish man to thank God that he was not made a Gentile, a slave, or a woman.

William Barclay states that it is not only remarkable that women should appear in Matthew's genealogy, but also one should look at who these woman happened to be. Rahab was the harlot of Jericho (Joshua 2:1-7). Ruth was not even a Jewess, but a Moabite (Ruth

1:4), even though the law states in Deuteronomy 23:3 that "a Moabite shall not enter into the congregation of the Lord, even to their tenth generation they shall not enter into the congregation of the Lord for ever." Ruth belonged to a hated and alien people. Tamar was a deliberate seducer and an adulteress (Genesis 38). Bathsheba was the woman that David seduced from Uriah, her husband, with an unforgivable cruelty (2 Samuel 11, 12). Barclay concludes, "If Matthew had ransacked the pages of the Old Testament for improbable candidates he could not have discovered four more incredible ancestors for Jesus Christ."[1]

At the very beginning of his Gospel, Matthew shows us, in a very symbolic manner, that in the gospel of Jesus Christ barriers are coming down. This is not business as usual; in the coming of Christ there is something new and revolutionary taking place. Matthew, at the very beginning, is stating in graphic terms that the grace and love of God in Jesus Christ are universal — for everyone. The old, contemptible barriers between men and women are gone; each is equally dear to God and to God's purpose. The remarkable thing is that Ruth, so unconscious of her role in history, through the ordinary and mundane happenings of everyday life, is able to contribute to the universal aspects of the grace of God. A non-Israelite woman, considered to be foreign, unclean, and ungodly, helps to make it possible for the boundaries of God's kingdom to be expanded so as to include all people.

There are no territorial boundaries to God's love and concern. Jacob, after he awakens from his dream of the ladder, looks back on his experience and declares, "Surely God is in this place and I did not know it." He had narrowed the limits on the territory where God could care for him and now God pushes the boundaries out further and further. Peter had some strange ideas as to who was and was not in the kingdom. Then one day at the home of Cornelius he had a dream regarding animals that were let down in a sheet before him. In that dream he discovered that in God's creation all that God has made is good, and Peter's boundaries were expanded to include all people.

The presence of Ruth's name in Matthew's genealogy at the beginning of the New Testament symbolically impresses on our minds that God is ever expanding our boundaries. But, our world is ever seeking to classify, limit, divide, restrict, confine, and belittle individuals. In our nation there is grave concern about the increase in the number of hate crimes, especially those resulting from race and sexual orientation. We must never forget that the work of the Kingdom of God is to expand the boundaries and obliterate the barriers. One of the great lessons in Paul's life was his discovery that in Jesus Christ there are no boundaries. The apostle asserts that in Christ there is neither Jew nor Greek, there is neither slave nor free, neither male nor female, for all are one in Christ Jesus, heirs according to the promise. In Christ men and women have entered into the freedom of becoming sons and daughters of God.

The apostle reminds us in 2 Corinthians 5:18 that God "has given us this ministry of reconciliation." The stretching of our hands to our brothers and sisters in Christ will of necessity cross over every human barrier and obstacle. Jesus is cosmic; he is not the private possession of any people. The gospel is global, not the possession of any nation or culture. In Christ the barriers are gone because the fears are gone. It is fear that erects barriers and builds walls of hostility. Are we as Christians contributing to the world's divisiveness or to its healing? Are we building barriers instead of removing them? Are we providing answers to the world's problems, or have we become part of the problem? Sometimes it causes me to wonder. I cannot help but think about all of our brothers and sisters, in all parts of the world today, who are giving their lives to the tearing down and removal of barriers. The tragedy is that many church people through their behavior and actions are perpetuating the very walls that others are giving their lives to eradicate.

Expanding boundaries, removing barriers, being involved in the "ministry of reconciliation," that is our God-given task. But it is risky and serious business. It got Jesus into serious trouble that led all the way to Golgotha. When Parliament in Cape Town, South Africa, passed legislation giving the government the power to forbid interracial services, the Anglican Dean in Cape Town placed on the door of St. George's Cathedral a notice bearing these words: *This Cathedral is open to all men and women, of all races, to all services, at all times.* The Dean of the cathedral was arrested, convicted, and placed in prison. Removing barriers got him into serious trouble. Just think of it, Jesus drew a circle so wide that it included you and me. God accepts us for what we are — sinners in need of the grace of God in Jesus Christ. We need to make sure that our circles are wide enough to include all of God's children.

This has been driven home to us once again in the brutal murder of Matthew Shepard. He was tied to a fence post on a Wyoming farm and pistol-whipped to death by two men because he was gay. There was a great outpouring of grief, pain, and anger across the country as massive numbers of people gathered in vigils and memorial services to comfort one another and to express their outrage at this heinous crime of hate. Tom Troeger, Professor of Preaching at the United Methodist Iliff School of Theology in Denver, preaching a resurrection service in the Episcopal tradition for Matthew Shepard, told about a poignant event that took place when he was in second grade. He said they had played the children's game, "You're out, you're out, you can't come in." He said he was always on the outside, but one day Louise, one of the girls who was always in, gave him a big wink, dropped the hand of the boy next to her and invited him in. He said he ran as fast as he could and made it in. The game stopped dead, when the boy whose hand she dropped said to her, "You can't do that. If you do that *everyone* will come in." Sporting a big grin Louise answered, "I know." Troeger ended his sermon by saying, "God is like Louise."

Ruth, the young woman who came from the despised Moabites, was included in the genealogy of Jesus, thus symbolically contributing to the universality of God's love and grace. She contributed to the expanding of the boundaries and the tearing down of the barriers. It is said of Florence Nightingale that she would cross the Crimean battlefield at night carrying her lantern seeking to care for the wounded and dying. Whomever she came upon, friend or foe, she stopped to minister to his needs. As she was tending to a dying soldier he said to her, "You are Jesus to me." Let us go through our community being Jesus to other people.

---

1. William Barclay, *Commentary on Matthew, Volume 1*, p. 7.

*Proper 28* • *Pentecost 26* • *Ordinary Time 33*

# God Remembers

*1 Samuel 1:4-20*

---

**On these** opening pages of 1 Samuel we are introduced to a family drama. Here is the story of Elkanah and his two wives, Hannah and Peninnah. Immediately, we encounter the tension in this family which is a result of Hannah's barrenness. Hannah's husband loves her and treats her with kindness. When they traveled to Shiloh on the day of sacrifice, Elkanah would give portions to his wife Peninnah and to her sons and daughters, but he would give a double portion to Hannah, and the text tells us he did this because he loved her even though she was barren. The conflict in the story is the result of Peninnah's verbal abuse of Hannah. Peninnah would constantly chide and "provoke her severely" because of her barrenness. Every time they would go up together to the house of the Lord, Peninnah would criticize and scold Hannah for being barren. Hannah would be driven to tears by the constant belittling, feeling that she could not take it anymore. She was so upset that she lost her appetite and could not eat. Elkanah was not aware of the emotional strain that Hannah was under. He seemed to be totally out of touch with the seriousness of the situation. He reveals his lack of perception by saying to Hannah, "Why is your heart sad? Am I not more to you than ten sons?" Sadly, both lover and provoker treat Hannah as God-forsaken.

While they were worshiping at Shiloh, Hannah rose early in the morning and prayed to the Lord. In her distress and bitterness, Hannah took the initiative to bring her case to God. She assumed that the God of Israel might care for those who are hurting and are without status and power. So in her prayer she cried out and said to the Lord:

> *O Lord of hosts, if only you will look on the misery of your servant, and remember me, and not forget your servant, but give to your servant a male child, then I will set him before you as a nazarite until the day of his death.*

The priest Eli was sitting near the entrance of the sanctuary and he saw Hannah at prayer. He noticed that her lips moved but she did not seem to be speaking. Thinking she was drunk, he told her that she was making a drunken spectacle of herself and that she ought to get rid of the wine. Hannah explained to him that she was not drunk, and that she did not drink wine. She declared, "I am a woman deeply troubled ... pouring out my soul before the Lord." She begged Eli that she not be considered as a "worthless woman." Then Eli made a remarkable response to her by saying, "Go in peace; the God of Israel grant the petition you have made to him." But Eli had no idea what the child who resulted from this vow would mean to his own priestly family. Hannah left the temple much encouraged and feeling as though her prayer was going to make a difference. She was no longer sad, because she had placed her future in the hands of God. In due time Hannah bore a son and she named him Samuel. When he was weaned she brought the infant Samuel to the house of the Lord at Shiloh, and she presented him to the Lord, saying, "As long as he lives he is yours!" Little did she or Elkanah know that Samuel was to become a prophet, a mediator of God's word to all Israel.

Bruce Birch in his commentary states, "Throughout this drama, God is the determining power. It is God who has 'closed her womb' (vv. 5-6); it is God to whom Hannah prays and makes her vow (vv. 10-11); it is God whom Eli invokes to grant Hannah's petition (v. 17); it is God who 'remembers' Hannah and grants her request (v. 19); it is God to whom the child, Samuel, is given in service (vv. 27-28). God works providentially in the events of this story."[1]

At the point of our discouragement, despair, and disappointment is the place of God's beginning. It is not in getting the right spiritual discipline or the latest strategic planning process that will meet our needs. As Hannah reveals, it is in simply and straightforwardly expressing our need to God. In doing so, Hannah recognized that wholeness in her life lay beyond those things that she can and cannot control and rested in God as the larger reality in life.

In Hannah's darkest hour, she came to the house of the Lord in Shiloh and "poured her soul out to God." She defined herself as "a woman deeply troubled." She felt, because of her barrenness, that many looked upon her as "a worthless woman." She explained to Eli, "I have been speaking out of my great anxiety and vexation all of this time." She cried out in her misery, saying to the Lord, "Remember me."

Many have felt the same anxiety and vexation that Hannah felt. The barrenness that you labor under may be the lack of accomplishment and achievement. One's sense of "worthlessness" can result from the inability to reach one's goals and ambitions, instead experiencing constant defeat and setback. The unkind words and caustic criticism of others, like Hannah constantly received from Peninnah, can cause you to weep and lose your appetite, as Hannah did. How easy it is to slip into an attitude of "worthlessness." But this is a story of God's grace coming to Hannah at the darkest moment of her life. It can also be the story of God's grace for us. It is the story of a dynamic grace that can transform the future and bring hope amid despair and pain. God remembered Hannah! In her darkest moment she made her greatest discovery. God did not forget her. God heard her cry, sensed her misery, and answered her prayer. What God did for Hannah, God can do for you.

We learn from Hannah the persistence that is needed to claim God's grace. Hannah was persistent because she felt she had lost God's attention, which is reflected in her prayer, "O Lord of hosts, if only you will look on the misery of your servant, and remember me" (1:11). Jesus taught us that we already have God's attention, and God is aware of our need. In the Sermon on the Mount Jesus declared, "Your Father knows what you need before you ask him" (Matthew 6:8). Job felt that he did not have God's attention. Out of his pain and anguish he cried, "O that I knew where I might find him!" Habakkuk, the prophet, felt that he did not have God's attention. He wanted to know where he could find God amid such injustice and violence. He cried, "O Lord, how long shall I cry for help and thou wilt not hear?" His book begins with a deep sigh and a heavy heart. God appeared to the prophet as inattentive. Both men discovered what Hannah discovered — that God is neither remote nor reluctant.

The fact is that God is not far removed from any of us. God is not disinterested to the point that we need to go begging and pleading for his concern. What is needed on our part is not a relentless beating on the door of heaven, but just for us to know that God is. God cares. God remembers. E. Stanley Jones tells about the prayer of a little girl who was the daughter of a missionary friend in India. She prayed, "God bless my parents, and my brother and sister, my friends and our world. And now, God, take care of yourself, for if anything ever happens to you, we'd be in a terrible mess." She knew that God was near and attentive. She shared with God her greatest concern. However, Hannah reveals to us that there is a trustful persistence that is required to claim God's grace.

Hannah's story presents us with a simple yet profound theme: prayer will quiet and comfort the most troubled heart. Hannah admitted to Eli that she was a "woman deeply troubled." She was troubled and tormented from without by the taunts of Peninnah. She was tormented from within by her own doubts of her own self-esteem that was being torn down by Peninnah's constant jeers regarding her barrenness. She had strong doubts about herself to the point that she was concerned that people would judge her worthless. She was the victim of jealousy and misunderstanding. But something remarkable happened. She came to the house of the Lord in Shiloh and poured out her heart to God in prayer. Following her prayer Eli said to her, "Go in peace." She was no longer downcast and "her countenance was sad no longer." After all of her troubles she found peace. Many times it is the offering of prayer, not the answer to prayer, that brings peace. Peace is not the result of God answering prayer, but peace comes in the very act of turning to God in the first place. Hannah did not know if she would get an answer to her prayer, she did not know the outcome, but one thing she did know: God remembered her, and God listened as she poured out her soul. She encountered God in prayer and she had found peace.

Where did Hannah make her discovery of God? Right in the midst of everyday life. She cried out right where she was amid her despair. Richard Foster in his book *Prayer* reminds us that "the discovery of God lies in the daily and ordinary, not in the spectacular and heroic. If we cannot find God in the routine of home and shop, then we will not find him at all. Ours is to be a symphonic piety in which all the activities of work and play and family and worship and sex and sleep are the holy habitats of the eternal."[2] We cannot clean ourselves up and come to God. That is the very thing we cannot do, but God comes to us where we are. God comes to us on the level of our need. That is the meaning of the incarnation: God comes to us on the level of our need, looks us squarely in the eye, and asks, "Where does it hurt and how can I help?" Hannah prayed to God in the midst of her troubled life, and it was there that she encountered God in prayer and she was no longer sad.

After Eli admonished Hannah to go in peace, he assured her that not only did God hear her prayer, but also that the God of Israel would grant the request she made. In due time she had a son, and he was named Samuel. She brought the infant to the house of worship and presented him to the Lord. Hannah told the Lord that Samuel was God's for as long as he lived. Hannah's response to the gift of God's grace was to give back what she had received. We too must give back the grace we have received. This would include worship, which is the giving back of grace as praise. We are the recipients of God's grace so that we may become the dispensers, the givers of grace. If we attempt to keep grace as a possession, we will lose it. God's grace was manifested to Hannah in the person of Samuel, and he brought much blessing to her, as well as ending the plight of her barrenness and the disgraceful and hurtful taunting of Peninnah. Because Hannah gave back this gift of grace to God, Samuel would bring a blessing to the entire country of Israel. Bruce Birch reminds us "that we, with the community of faith, must become less concerned over who and how many have received God's grace and more concerned with the ways to which God's grace is given back into God's service."[3] Also, it is Jesus who reminds us, "From everyone to whom much has been given, much will be required; and from the one to whom much has been entrusted, even more will be demanded" (Luke 12:48b).

---

1. Bruce Birch in *New Intrepeter's Bible, Volume 2*, p. 973.

2. Richard Foster, *Prayer*, p. 171.

3. Birch, *op. cit.*, p. 978.

*Christ The King Sunday*

# What's So Great About Jesus?

*2 Samuel 23:1-7*

---

**Today is the** festival of Christ the King. During this past year our liturgical cycle has moved from the whole world waiting for its Savior, through the coming of an infant in poverty and obscurity, his dying, rising, and returning to the Father, the church's own pilgrimage in the image of Christ, to his final coming trailing on clouds of glory. Today we reach the liturgical end of the story. Today our liturgy celebrates the high point of creation, when humankind and all that is, even death itself, will be subjected to Christ. This is so clearly expressed by the apostle Paul when he wrote, "When he hands over the kingdom to God the Father after he has destroyed every ruler and every authority and power" (1 Corinthians 15:24). Walter J. Burghardt states: "At the close of the church year, the celebration of Christ the King is like the *coda* in a Beethoven symphony. It not only brings the movement to a decisive end, but it forms a climax to what has gone before it. It is at once a summing up and at the same time splendidly new."[1]

The text in 2 Samuel 23:1-7 is a poem, and this poem and the one by Hannah in 1 Samuel 2:1-10 serve as lyrical-theological affirmations that bracket the entire story of David and kingship. This poem articulates God's resolve to have an "anointed king," as well as God's purpose to use the anointed one to bring well-being and to raise up a king congenial to God's purpose. Therefore, these three motifs — God's sovereign power (vv. 1-2); God's moral expectation (v. 3), and God's abiding fidelity (v. 5) provide the clues to the shape and significance of David's rule. Brueggemann points out that "this high royal theology is taken up and used by the early church for christological affirmation. The New Testament found this language readily appropriate for Jesus — who is raised to power, who ruled justly, and who bears God's abiding commitment."[2] As we look through the lens of our text it brings into focus more clearly the significance of our celebration of Christ the King Sunday.

A grandmother wanted her granddaughter to attend Sunday school. So she arranged to pick her up and take her. She took her to her class and introduced her to her teacher. Following the class the grandmother picked her up and drove her home. The grandmother was anxious to hear about her granddaughter's experience. She noticed that her granddaughter was in a rather pensive mood as she silently stared out of the car window. Finally, the grandmother could not stand the suspense any longer and asked her granddaughter, "Well, what did you think of Sunday school?" Thoughtfully, she replied, "Grandma, what's so great about Jesus?"

People ask that same question today. They wonder why Christians are making such a fuss about Jesus. Why all of the commotion? Why all of the excitement, celebration, and festivity? Why all of the contatas, concerts, and pageants?

How would you answer that question? If your child or grandchild would ask you that question, how would you respond? I have thought a great deal about this question. I realize that we would probably have as many answers as we have people in church today. Each of us has come to Christ by a different road or pathway. There is a vast variety of religious experiences. Since your answer would relate to your own personal experience of Jesus in your life, you can see how our answers would be so varied.

Today we are completing our liturgical journey that has encompassed the entire life of Jesus. In our journey we have reflected on the birth of Jesus, and our journey through Epiphany and Lent has given us a better idea of the kind of world that he lived in. We have discovered that the land of Palestine at the time of Jesus' birth was controlled by the Roman Empire. Two thirds of that empire were slaves. They were sold as property, and punished and killed at the discretion of their owners. Magicians and soothsayers abounded in the land. Barbarous struggles between men and beasts were the most popular form of entertainment. In a month's time 20,000 lives were sacrificed in the Roman arena. The worship of the gods was based on fear and superstition. The vices of the gods became the virtues of men and women, and they lived in terror of the gods. The masses were haunted rather than helped by their religion.

What is so great about Jesus is that he brought a revolutionary understanding of God into a world that did not have the slightest concept of a God as loving and considerate. Jesus revealed a good and loving God, who is the creator of the heavens and the earth, and all of this creation is good. Jesus' central theme is "God so loved the world" — a love that is for everyone and everything. God is concerned for all the people of the earth. God is the God of Abraham, Isaac, and Jacob, as well as the God of Sarah, Leah, and Rachel. Not only did Jesus provide us a new concept of a loving God, but also he showed us a God who loves and cares for all.

In this liturgical year we have discovered many encounters that Jesus had, but none is more interesting than his encounter with Philip. It takes place in John 14 where Philip says to Jesus, "Lord, show us the Father." Jesus said to him, "Have I been with you so long, and yet you do not know me, Philip? He who has seen me has seen the Father ... I am in the Father and the Father in me." What kind of heavenly Father do we see in Jesus? We see one who is willing to socialize and eat with sinners. Jesus enjoys the company of people, regardless of who they were, so much so that he was called by his critics a winebibbler and a glutton. He associates with social outcasts like Zacchaeus, who was a quisling, who sold out to the Roman government so as to get an important tax job. He comes to the lonely and the forgotten as seen in his visit to the man at the pool of Bethesda who for 38 years lay at the edge of the pool unable to get in the water because he had no one to help him. He reaches out to the prostitutes and the lepers. He gives sight to the blind and makes the lame to walk. He ministers to a family that is humiliated and socially disgraced because the wine ran out at their daughter's wedding. Jesus was sensitive to their embarrassment and he helped them. In our liturgical journey through the church year this is the kind of heavenly Father that Jesus has come to reveal to us. That's what is so great about Jesus!

The story of the New Testament forever is reminding us that God has come among us in the person of Jesus to share our lives. Regarding that fact there is no doubt. Jesus' coming was so different from the world of the Greek and Roman gods that it was hard for the masses to understand God in these terms. As Bishop Robinson reminded us in his penetrating book *Honest to God,* God is not out there, or up there, but God is here with us. The life of Jesus is the fact of God's friendship. Jesus was made of woman under the law. God through Christ came in the midst of life, as expressed by the apostle Paul in the text, "in Christ God was reconciling the world to himself." In the words of E. Stanley Jones, "Jesus has domesticated God." He moves into our total life from the living room to the boardroom, to the sickroom, to the bedroom, to the courtroom. God is with us from the nursery to the nursing home, from the obstetrician to the funeral director. This is absolutely remarkable; never has the world known God in such terms. That's what's so great about Jesus: God is with us every step of the way.

When we come to celebrate the kingship of Christ, it is not political kingship. Jesus reminded us, "My kingdom is not of this world" (John 18:36). Burghardt stated that through the birth of Jesus a trinity of tyrants, Satan, sin, and death, were defeated by the lordship of Christ. Not that they have vanished from the earth, but their despotic power has been broken. We need no longer be slaves to Satan and sin. Jesus did not defeat them by the force of arms, nor by power or pomp, but by dying and rising. How appropriate are the apostle's words:

> *We do not live to ourselves and we do not die to ourselves. If we live, we live to the Lord, and if we die, we die to the Lord; so then, whether we live or whether we die, we are the Lord's. For to this end Christ died and lived again, so that he might be the Lord of both the dead and the living.* —Romans 14:7-9

Jesus is "the king of hearts." He draws us to himself not by might nor by power, but this King draws us to himself by the cords of love. The road that leads us to God's kingdom of love and grace does not pass through corporate boardrooms or political caucuses. It passes through the cross.

---

1. Walter J. Burghardt, *Still Proclaiming Your Wonders*, p. 74.

2. Walter Brueggemann, *Interpretation*, "First and Second Samuel," p. 347.

*All Saints' Sunday*

# With All
# The Saints

*Isaiah 25:6-9*

---

Isaiah 25 is a remarkable passage for All Saints' Sunday. It begins with an outburst of praise for what God has done and for what God will do. An unidentified city — strong, oppressive and hostile — will be destroyed and never rebuilt. Amid the destruction God protects and cares for the poor and the needy. Once this evil city and its ruthless inhabitants have been destroyed and vanish, another city will rise on Mount Zion where God will invite all people to a magnificent feast. God will wipe away all tears, he will swallow up death forever, and the disgrace of his people he will take away from all the earth. Then all the people will rejoice saying, "This is the Lord for whom we have waited; let us be glad and rejoice in his salvation" (v. 9). In this passage we have a glimpse of what God has done, what God is doing, and what God will do. On All Saints' Day it gives us an opportunity to reflect on the struggle of the saints in the past and how we are benefactors of their struggles and triumphs. It reminds us that with the earlier saints we have the same goal and aspirations as we too struggle in our search for "the city that has foundations, whose architect and builder is God" (Hebrews 11:10).

With the arrival of fall the football season is now in full swing. The fall mania is upon us. The marching bands, the huge crowds flocking to the stadium, the excitement of the play on the gridiron, all add up to this electrifying experience we Americans call football. For the next several weeks wives are going to lose contact with their husbands. Every favor that a wife asks of her husband will be answered the same way for the next several months: "Wait until this next play is over." One husband said to his wife as he turned on the television for the first game of the season, "Dear, do you have any final words before the season begins?" One wife had all she could stand of football. She turned off the television, stood in front of it, and crossed her arms, saying to her husband, "I believe you love football more than you love me." The husband thought for a moment and then said, "But I love you more than volleyball."

Football has changed a great deal since I played high school football in the fifties. We used the single wing formation, something that most people know nothing about today. The most significant change over the years has been the deployment of two separate teams, one for offense and one for defense. In my high school days, as a varsity player one was expected to play offensively and defensively. It was not uncommon for a player to play the entire game. Today the modern football player is either an offensive or defensive specialist. Even the cheerleaders have a set of cheers for each team. When the defensive team is on the field they shout, "Hold that line! Hold that line!" But when the offensive teams takes over they yell out, "Go, team, go! Go, team, go!"

There was a moment when Jesus faced his disciples. Behind him were all the years of public ministry, the trials and the triumphs, the ecstasy and the agony. All the previous events culminated in this moment as he stood before his disciples, a strange and motley mixture of human beings, and said, "Go therefore and make disciples of all nations, baptizing them in the name of the Father and of the Son and of the Holy Spirit" (Matthew 28:19). Along with this challenge there was a promise, "And remember, I am with you always, to the end of the age" (v. 20b).

The saints who came before us were offensively-minded. They moved the ball down the field. Look what happened. It was like the concentric circles which result from a rock thrown into a pool of water. First there were twelve, then in the Upper Room 120, then 3,000 at the day of Pentecost after Peter preached his sermon. For four centuries the Christian fellowship was a mighty force and power that no emperor or nation could stop. But today a malaise has come over the church. It has become defensive, producing a fortress mentality, a kind of spiritual protectionism. There is a widespread desire to hold, protect, and keep what we have by avoiding risk. The cry is, "Hold that line!" Let's stop the clock, call a time out, re-group, huddle, and do some serious thinking together. Let's consider one important question. How did we get here? We got here because the saints before us were willing to carry the ball forward. Take a stethoscope and listen to the heartbeat of the early church. What do you discover? J.B. Phillips in his introduction to his book, *The Young Church in Action,* states:

> *Here we see Christianity, the real thing, in action for the first time in human history. The young church is appealing in its simplicity and singlemindedness. Here we see the church ... valiant and unspoiled — a body of ordinary men and women joined in an unconquerable fellowship never before seen on the earth ... There is someone at work here besides mere human beings ... never before has any small body of ordinary people so moved the world that their enemies could say with tears in their eyes, that these men and women "have turned the world upside down."*

We got to where we are because of the readiness of these saints to believe, to obey, to give, to suffer, and if need be to die, so as to establish a way of fellowship united in love and faith. They were open to the God-ward side of life that is almost unknown to us today. Their rallying cry was never, "Hold that line," but rather, "Go, church, go!"

Take that stethoscope again and place it at the heartbeat of the church in the Dark Ages. The heartbeat is weak and nearly gone. What has happened to the church? It has grown fat and short of breath through prosperity and wealth, losing its vibrancy and power. After Constantine it became accommodating to the Roman Empire. It became comfortable and cozy with the culture and politics. The story is told that Pope Leo X took Erasmus, the humanist of Rotterdam, to view the treasury of the church. Leo said to Erasmus as he opened the door to the church's vast holdings, "Never again will the church have to say, 'Silver and gold have I not.' " Whereupon Erasmus answered, "Neither can it say, 'In the name of Jesus Christ rise up and walk.' "

Then on the scene came a young monk named Martin Luther, who was teaching theology at Wittenberg College in Germany. It was on this very weekend at the end of October in 1517, that he nailed the Ninety-Five Theses to the door of Wittenberg College, declaring a debate in regard to the church's sale of indulgences. This marked the beginning of the Protestant Reformation.

This lowly monk challenged the mighty church and its papacy. A synod was called by the church in the town of Worms in order to deal with this iconoclastic young priest. Assembled in this small German town were Emperor Charles V, representatives of the papacy in Rome, and the brilliant John Eck, the papal legate who sought to interrogate Luther. Eck asked Luther, "Do you repudiate your books and the errors they contain?" There was dead silence as everyone waited for Luther's reply. This simple monk, a miner's son, with nothing to sustain him but his own faith in the word of God, answered, "I will not recant anything, for to go against conscience is neither right nor safe. Here I stand, I cannot do otherwise. God help me!" Carlyle called this "the greatest moment in the modern history of the world." The church historian Roland Bainton declared that this event was like lighting a match in a tinderbox. It spread like wildfire across Germany, Europe, and England and eventually to the new world. The rallying cry was, "Go, church, go!"

How do you think the Methodists got here? It was the direct result of men and women who had the fervor and enthusiasm of a Francis Asbury who carried the ball against stiff odds and a rugged opponent. Asbury covered over 270,000 miles on horseback across wilderness trials. Asbury crossed and recrossed the Allegheny Mountains more than sixty times. He traveled from Maine to Virginia, through the Carolinas, wading through swamps, swimming the rivers that flowed down the eastern slopes of the Alleghenies to the Atlantic, on down to Georgia. On numerous occasions he was so sick and exhausted he had to tie himself to the saddle. When he became the episcopal leader of the Methodist Church in 1784, the church only had a few thousand members. At the time of his death in 1816, the Methodist Church had more than 200,000 members, at that time the largest Protestant church in America.

We are where we are because of the saints who carried the ball. These saints were not passive or defensive. They did not shout, "Hold that line!" Rather, they were inspired by the rallying cry, "Go, church, go!" They did go and they conquered in the name of the risen Christ. We are inspired by those who have fought the fight of faith before us. They faced difficult odds and their accomplishments were the result of difficult struggles. Jesus in the most critical moment of his life struggled with the possibilities of a very painful future. In the garden as he was praying he knew the consequences of what lay ahead. In all honesty he cried out to the Father, "Allow this cup to pass from me." Jesus was saying, "I don't want to die." He struggled with the words, "Let it be possible." He conquered with the words, "Not my will but yours be done." In thinking about the saints who went before us we realize what a great heritage we have received, and we have the responsibility of passing it on to those who come after us. We find ourselves as a vital link that connects the past with the future. We face our struggles as they faced theirs. However, we are facing new struggles that our forefathers and mothers never had to face. We are facing very complex problems and issues resulting from our hi-tech society as we enter a new millenium. But there is one thing that remains the same, as it did for Jesus and Christians in every age: we all will conqueror with Jesus' words, "Father, not what I want, but what you want" (Mark 14:36).

Just like Isaiah said, we are glad and rejoice in the God of our salvation — for all that God has done, for all that God is doing, for all that God will do.

*Thanksgiving Day*

# Thankful Living

*Joel 2:21-27*

---

**Joel informs** the people of Judah that God has willed that humankind should have abundant life. This abundant life is characterized by good relationships with others, with all of God's creation, as well as the land and all its creatures. He points out that this abundant life of relationships is possible by first having a harmonious relationship with God. The prophet warns Judah if they desert God, making God unnecessary, and turn to other sources for life, then Judah is faced with hopelessness and the threat of annihilation.

The prophet informs Judah that when God's salvation comes, nature too will be healed. Peace with God brings a peace with all that God has made. One cannot be at peace with God and live in conflict or discord with what God has created. Joel admonishes the soil to be glad and rejoice, and the animals in the field not to fear; the pastures will turn green, and the vines and the trees will again bear their yield. God will again give the usual "early" rain in October and November and the "later" rains in March and April, as God has always done before. Joel declares that Judah's response to all of this is to "praise the name of the Lord your God, who has dealt wondrously with you" (v. 26b). In other words, practice thankful living.

Our thanksgiving and gratitude should be seen by the manner of our everyday living, how we respond to the good things that God has provided for us. A child shows not only appreciation, but respect for his parents by the way the child uses what the parents have provided for him or her. There is no way that a child could repay parents for all that they do. Parents do not expect to be repaid. All that parents desire from their children is gratitude and appreciation, not so much in words but reflected in thankful living. I think the same is true of God, who provides us with all of the beneficial gifts of creation. To use these gifts recklessly and carelessly is to disrespect not only the gift but the giver. When we take it upon ourselves to obliterate what God has wrought it is like spitting in the face of God. There is a Jewish folk tale regarding two men fighting over a piece of land. Each claimed ownership. To resolve their differences, they agreed to put the case before a rabbi. The rabbi listened but could not come to a decision. Finally, he said, "Since I cannot decide to whom this land belongs, let us ask the land." He put his ear to the ground, then straightened up, "Gentlemen, the land says that it belongs to neither of you — but that you belong to it." Henri Nouwen expresses this so well:

> *Gratitude is a response to grace. The compassionate life is a grateful life, and actions born out of gratefulness are not compulsive but free, not somber but joyful, not fanatical but liberating. When gratitude is the source of our actions, our giving becomes receiving and those to whom we minister become our ministers.*[1]

On Thanksgiving Day we gather to worship and offer our thanksgiving to God for God's bountiful goodness to us. How ironic that we express this in songs that talk about plowing, sowing, and reaping. We sing about the harvest home of wheat, corn, and grain. With nostalgic feelings our thoughts go back to the land and animals, the very things that we know so little about today. Tillich reminds us that " we have so secluded ourselves in human superiority, in intellectual arrogance, in a domineering attitude toward nature, to where we are incapable of perceiving the harmonious sounds of nature."[2] Our deafness toward nature has tragically caused an enmity between humankind and nature, between nature and nature which makes thanksgiving, on our part, almost impossible. To the earth it's tough to sing those thanksgiving hymns when we realize what we have done through the greed of our commercialism and consumerism. Somehow we Christians have come to believe that creation and every created creature is to serve human need. We have developed a warped theology that has supported the idea that humans are superior to nature, even contemptuous of it, encouraging the use of nature for our slightest whims. How can we express our thanksgiving to God for something we have so tragically misused?

What on earth are we to do? First, we can begin our thanksgiving by affirming God as creator. This is the affirmation that we make in the Apostles' Creed: "I believe in God, the Father Almighty, maker of heaven and earth!" That's a powerful statement. Affirming God as creator means affirming that creation belongs to God. This is a good starting point for a Christian thanksgiving response for the earth's environment. Contrary to popular belief, and regardless of what corporations happen to think, humanity cannot own creation. The psalmist declares in Psalm 24:1, "The earth is the Lord's and the fullness thereof."

This simple truth echoes throughout the pages of the Bible. God answers Job, "Whatever is under the whole heaven is mine." Before God gave the Ten Commandments to Moses, God said, "All the earth is mine." The Bible is clear that the earth came forth by the power of God. The apostle Paul reminds us "that in God we live, move and have our being." On Thanksgiving Day this is where we begin. This is our starting point.

As we go about our work in the church of caring for souls, feeding the poor, and caring for the homeless, at the same time our actions must guard, protect, preserve, and uphold God's purpose for creation. We must go about our ministries in a manner of thankful living by ever affirming that God is creator and sustainer and that we are the creatures, caretakers, and stewards. One hymn that sets the mood for a day of thanksgiving is:

> *This is my Father's world,*
> *O let me ne'er forget*
> *That though the wrong seems oft so strong,*
> *God is the ruler yet.*

Second, let us thank God for a creation that is good. We begin by remembering that the biblical view of creation is that it is good, simply because it is the work of God. The goodness of creation is underscored in Genesis 1. God saw that it was "good." The words are continually repeated. After the appearance of water, land, plants, and light, God said, "It is good." After the appearance of fish, birds, and land animals again God said, "It is good." After the creation of man and woman God said, "It is very good." Frances Alexander's hymn is so appropriate,

> *All things bright and beautiful,*
> *All creatures great and small,*
> *All things wise and wonderful:*
> *The Lord God made them all.*

There have been times in the history of the church when Christians sought to escape from the world, feeling that physical and fleshly things were tainted and sinful. There is not the slightest evidence of this in the creation account in Genesis. The Bible tells us how God cares for and rejoices in God's creation. In Matthew 6, God feeds the birds; a sparrow does not fall from the nest without God noticing it. God clothes the lilies of the fields. In Psalm 104, God calls every star by name. In Isaiah 65, God rejoices in all God has made. All things created are a source of enjoyment and glory to God. Here is the source of our praise and thanksgiving.

The crowning point of the goodness of God's creation is expressed in John 1:14 when "the Word became flesh." The incarnation of God in the flesh is the greatest evidence of the goodness of the physical and human world. The highest revelation of God was obtained through the physical birth of a child. God entered the world through the world's process of birth. Through this human birth of Jesus Christ the word became so transparent, that Jesus could say, "He who has seen me has seen the Father." In the incarnation God entered all created reality, even nature. The coming of God through Christ is the final answer to any thought that the flesh is evil. Thank God for a creation that is "very good."

Third, let us affirm our thanksgiving by affirming our love for the God of creation. Could you take any thing that is precious and meaningful to someone you love and who loves you and destroy it? If we love God how can we have disregard for God's creation? Because God has created the earth, it has a worth all of it own.

> *This is my Father's world ...*
> *His hand the wonders wrought.*

Creation is precious because of the one who has given it to us. The quality of our thanksgiving, compassion, and concern extends to even the animals of the land. We do not equate animals with people, but when they are killed for human necessity it is done with the least amount of suffering. As Christians we use animals in ways to conserve their dignity. This is part of our thankful living.

The biblical point is clear. Although God gives us dominion over the earth, that dominion is clearly limited. God did say in Genesis 1:28, "Be fruitful and multiply, and fill the earth and subdue it." This is a clear biblical mandate, but one that is conditional and limited. Human rights to use the earth are limited by God's right of ownership. God's right of ownership is absolute. Our use of the earth is conditional. All creation, all of those things that our thanksgiving hymns speak about — seed, harvest, grain, and animals — result from an act of God's grace. The gifts of creation are unmerited; they represent God's goodness to us. Our response to such unmerited goodness should be one not only of thanksgiving and praise with our lips, but also one of lives that culminate in thankful everyday living.

---

1. Henri Nouwen, *A Reflection On The Christian Life,* p. 126.

2. Paul Tillich, *Shaking The Foundations.*

# Lectionary Preaching After Pentecost

The following index will aid the user of this book in matching the correct Sunday with the appropriate text during Pentecost. All texts in this book are from the series for Lesson One, Revised Common Lectionary. (Note that the ELCA division of Lutheranism is now following the Revised Common Lectionary.) The Lutheran and Roman Catholic designations indicate days comparable to Sundays on which Revised Common Lectionary Propers are used.

**(Fixed dates do not pertain to Lutheran Lectionary)**

| Fixed Date Lectionaries<br>*Revised Common (including ELCA)*<br>*and Roman Catholic* | Lutheran Lectionary<br>*Lutheran* |
|---|---|
| The Day of Pentecost | The Day of Pentecost |
| The Holy Trinity | The Holy Trinity |
| May 29-June 4 — Proper 4, Ordinary Time 9 | Pentecost 2 |
| June 5-11 — Proper 5, Ordinary Time 10 | Pentecost 3 |
| June 12-18 — Proper 6, Ordinary Time 11 | Pentecost 4 |
| June 19-25 — Proper 7, Ordinary Time 12 | Pentecost 5 |
| June 26-July 2 — Proper 8, Ordinary Time 13 | Pentecost 6 |
| July 3-9 — Proper 9, Ordinary Time 14 | Pentecost 7 |
| July 10-16 — Proper 10, Ordinary Time 15 | Pentecost 8 |
| July 17-23 — Proper 11, Ordinary Time 16 | Pentecost 9 |
| July 24-30 — Proper 12, Ordinary Time 17 | Pentecost 10 |
| July 31-Aug. 6 — Proper 13, Ordinary Time 18 | Pentecost 11 |
| Aug. 7-13 — Proper 14, Ordinary Time 19 | Pentecost 12 |
| Aug. 14-20 — Proper 15, Ordinary Time 20 | Pentecost 13 |
| Aug. 21-27 — Proper 16, Ordinary Time 21 | Pentecost 14 |
| Aug. 28-Sept. 3 — Proper 17, Ordinary Time 22 | Pentecost 15 |
| Sept. 4-10 — Proper 18, Ordinary Time 23 | Pentecost 16 |
| Sept. 11-17 — Proper 19, Ordinary Time 24 | Pentecost 17 |
| Sept. 18-24 — Proper 20, Ordinary Time 25 | Pentecost 18 |

| | |
|---|---|
| Sept. 25-Oct. 1 — Proper 21, Ordinary Time 26 | Pentecost 19 |
| Oct. 2-8 — Proper 22, Ordinary Time 27 | Pentecost 20 |
| Oct. 9-15 — Proper 23, Ordinary Time 28 | Pentecost 21 |
| Oct. 16-22 — Proper 24, Ordinary Time 29 | Pentecost 22 |
| Oct. 23-29 — Proper 25, Ordinary Time 30 | Pentecost 23 |
| Oct. 30-Nov. 5 — Proper 26, Ordinary Time 31 | Pentecost 24 |
| Nov. 6-12 — Proper 27, Ordinary Time 32 | Pentecost 25 |
| Nov. 13-19 — Proper 28, Ordinary Time 33 | Pentecost 26<br>Pentecost 27 |
| Nov. 20-26 — Christ the King | Christ the King |

---

Reformation Day (or last Sunday in October) is October 31 (Revised Common, Lutheran)

All Saints' Day (or first Sunday in November) is November 1 (Revised Common, Lutheran, Roman Catholic)

**Books In This Cycle B Series**

**GOSPEL SET**

*A God For This World*
Sermons for Advent/Christmas/Epiphany
Maurice A. Fetty

*The Culture Of Disbelief*
Sermons For Lent/Easter
Donna E. Schaper

*The Advocate*
Sermons For Sundays After Pentecost (First Third)
Ron Lavin

*Surviving In A Cordless World*
Sermons For Sundays After Pentecost (Middle Third)
Lawrence H. Craig

*Against The Grain — Words For A Politically Incorrect Church*
Sermons For Sundays After Pentecost (Last Third)
Steven E. Albertin

**FIRST LESSON SET**

*Defining Moments*
Sermons For Advent/Christmas/Epiphany
William L. Self

*From This Day Forward*
Sermons For Lent/Easter
Paul W. Kummer

*Out From The Ordinary*
Sermons For Sundays After Pentecost (First Third)
Gary L. Carver

*Wearing The Wind*
Sermons For Sundays After Pentecost (Middle Third)
Stephen M. Crotts

*Out Of The Whirlwind*
Sermons For Sundays After Pentecost (Last Third)
John A. Stroman

**SECOND LESSON SET**

*Humming Till The Music Returns*
Sermons For Advent/Christmas/Epiphany
Wayne Brouwer

*Ashes To Ascension*
Sermons For Lent/Easter
John A. Stroman

www.ingramcontent.com/pod-product-compliance
Lightning Source LLC
Chambersburg PA
CBHW071753040426
42446CB00012B/2539